USBORNE ACTIVITIES

Things to make for Mums

Rebecca Gilpin

Designed and illustrated by Non Figg,
Antonia Miller and Josephine Thompson

Steps illustrated by Molly Sage
Photographs by Howard Allman
Recipes by Catherine Atkinson

- 2   Painted butterflies card
- 4   Sparkly flower chains
- 6   Printed collage card
- 8   Tissue paper picture
- 10 Yummy chocolate truffles
- 12 Collage of your family
- 14 Decorated pot
- 16 Field of flowers painting
- 17 Printed wrapping paper
- 18 Flower chocolates
- 20 Flowery boxes
- 22 Cut-paper card
- 24 Paper flowers
- 26 Tiny decorated cakes
- 28 Painted stripes card
- 30 Shiny picture frame
- 32 Gift tag ideas

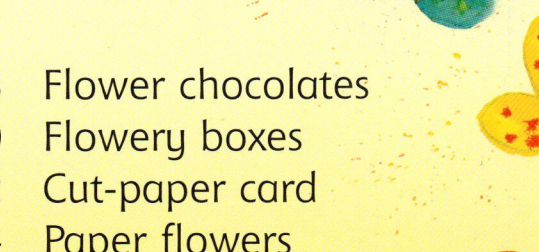

There are lots of bright stickers in the middle of this book.
You can use them to decorate the things you make.

Painted butterflies card

The paint needs to be watery.

1. Pour some blue paint onto an old plate and mix it with water. Then, use a small brush to paint butterfly wings, like this.

2. Wash your brush. Then, while the blue paint is wet, dab small dots of green paint onto it. The green paint will spread a little.

3. Leave the paint to dry. Then, paint a dark blue body in the middle of the wings. Add thin feelers to the top of the body.

4. Paint lots more butterflies. Try using orange and red paint together, and pink and yellow. Then, leave the paint to dry.

5. Make your painting into a card by folding a sheet of thick paper in half. Cut around the butterflies and glue them onto the card.

Leave a white border.

These butterflies have been splattered with paint (see below).

Splattering

Dip a dry brush into some runny paint. Then, pull a finger over the bristles, to splatter the paint over your picture.

Sparkly flower chains

Tape the flowers onto a window, so that the light shines through them.

1. Lay a large piece of plastic foodwrap on an old magazine. Then, rip two shades of pink tissue paper into lots of pieces.

2. Lay pieces of tissue paper on the foodwrap, overlapping each other. Cover as much of the foodwrap as you can.

3. Mix some PVA glue with water so that it is runny. Then, paint glue over the pieces of tissue paper, until they are covered.

4. Add another layer of tissue paper and glue. Then, add a third layer of paper and glue, and sprinkle glitter on the top.

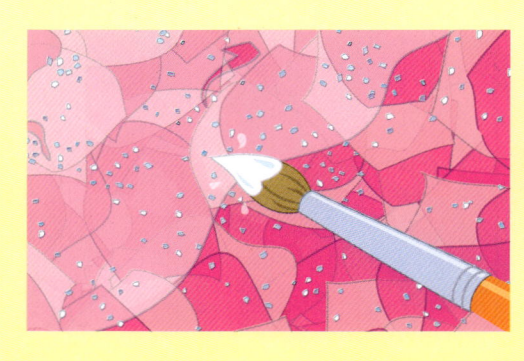

5. When the glue is dry, paint glue over the glitter and let it dry. Then, lay another piece of foodwrap on a newspaper.

6. Make layers of orange and yellow tissue paper and glue, as you did before. Add glitter and glue and leave it to dry.

4

You could make lots of chains and hang them up as a surprise for Mother's Day.

You could put sparkly flowers into a card so that they tumble out when it's opened.

7. Peel the glittery tissue paper off the foodwrap. Then, cut out pink flowers and small pink circles. Cut out some orange ones too.

8. Glue the orange circles onto the middle of the pink flowers. Glue pink circles onto the middle of the orange flowers.

9. Then, cut some thin ribbon into pieces which are different lengths and tape the flowers onto the ribbons, to make a chain.

5

Printed collage card

1. To make a card, cut a rectangle from thick paper and fold it in half. Then, cut another rectangle from thick cardboard.

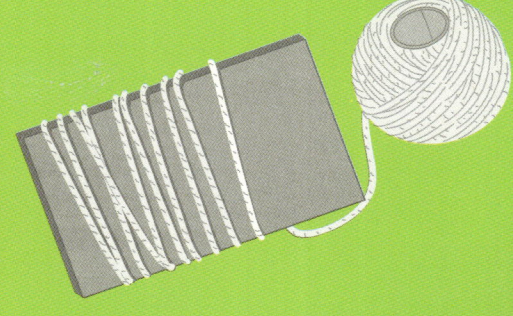

2. Tape the end of some string or wool to the cardboard. Then, wind the string roughly round and round, like this.

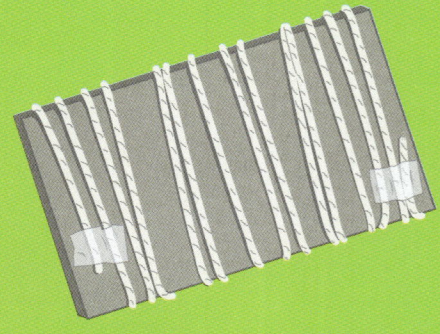

3. Wind the string all along the cardboard, then cut it. Tape the end on the same side of the cardboard as the other piece of tape.

4. Paint the string with yellow paint, so that it is covered. Then, press it onto the folded card, to print yellow lines.

5. Print more lines on the card, adding more paint as you go. Carry on until the card is covered in lots of yellow lines, like this.

Try cutting out lots of small flowers in different colours.

You could add some paper leaves and a stalk.

6. Cut a square from yellow paper, smaller than the card. Then, cut an even smaller square from light green paper.

7. Wrap string around another piece of cardboard. Then, print green lines on the green square, as you did before.

8. Glue the yellow and green squares onto the card. Then, cut out a white paper flower and a yellow middle, and glue them on.

7

Tissue paper picture

The strips are for the sides of the frame.

Use a glue stick.

1. Cut a rectangle from white tissue paper. Then, cut two cardboard strips which are a little longer than the tissue paper.

2. Glue the strips onto the sides of the tissue paper. Then, cut two strips which fit along the top and the bottom. Glue them on.

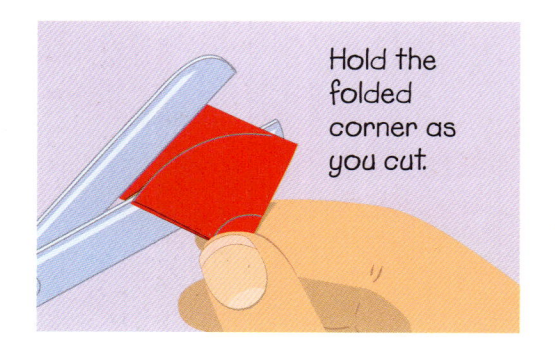

Hold the folded corner as you cut.

Draw curves like these for rounded petals.

Draw curves like these for pointed petals.

Folded corner

3. For a round flower, fold a square of tissue paper in half and in half again. Draw two curves and cut along them. Open out the flower.

4. Fold two squares of tissue paper in half, twice. Draw a curve on each one for the petals, then add another curve in the corner.

5. Cut along the lines, through all the layers of tissue paper, then open out the flowers. Then, cut out lots more flowers.

Glue more than one circle on some flowers.

Use a black felt-tip pen.

6. Glue the flowers onto the white tissue paper. Then, cut out little tissue paper circles and glue them in the middle of the flowers.

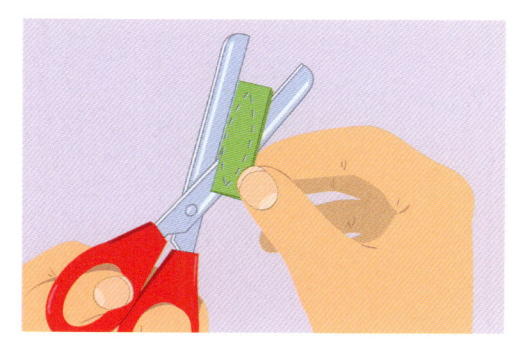

7. To make leaves, fold a strip of green tissue paper in half and then in half again. Cut a leaf shape through all the layers.

8. Glue the leaves in the gaps between the flowers. Then, draw outlines, spirals and petals on the flowers and lines on the leaves.

8

Tape the picture onto a window so that the light shines through it.

Yummy chocolate truffles

To make 12 truffles, you will need:

225g (8oz) white, milk or plain chocolate drops
4 tablespoons double cream
1 teaspoon of vanilla essence
4 tablespoons sugar strands
small paper cases

❀ These truffles need to be stored in an airtight container in a fridge and eaten within five days.

1. Pour about 3cm (1in) of water into a pan. Heat the pan until the water bubbles, then remove the pan from the heat.

2. Put the chocolate drops and cream into a heatproof bowl. Wearing oven gloves, carefully put the bowl into the pan.

You could give truffles to your mum in a flowery box (see pages 20-21).

Wear oven gloves.

3. Stir the chocolate and cream with a wooden spoon until the chocolate has melted. Carefully lift the bowl out of the water.

4. Leave the bowl to cool for 20 minutes, then stir in the vanilla. Put the mixture in a fridge for 1½ hours, until it is solid.

To make the number of truffles shown here you would need to make three times the mixture.

5. Put the sugar strands onto a plate. Scoop up some chocolate mixture with a teaspoon and put it in the sugar strands.

6. Using your fingers, roll the spoonful in the strands to make a ball. When it is covered, put it in a paper case. Make more truffles.

7. Put the truffles onto a plate. Then, put them in the fridge for at least 30 minutes, until they are completely hard.

11

Collage of your family
Girl

1. Cut a head and a neck from paper from an old magazine, then glue them onto a big piece of paper. Then, cut out a dress, too.

2. Glue on the dress, then cut arms and legs and glue them on, so they touch the dress. Cut out hands and glue them on, too.

3. Cut out some hair and glue it onto the head. Then, cut out red boots and glue them onto the girl's legs.

Make a collage of your family and pets, on blue paper. Then add lots of other things, like the sun, a house, a car and a bird.

You can make a boy in the same way as the girl – just cut out different hair and clothes.

Mother

4. Cut some yellow bows from paper and glue them onto the hair. Then, draw a face with black and red felt-tip pens.

1. Cut out a head, neck and some hair. Glue the hair onto the head and glue the head onto the big piece of paper. Then, draw a face.

This hair was made from two pieces of paper.

2. Cut out a top and a skirt and glue them onto the paper. Then, cut out arms, legs and shoes and glue them on, too.

Dog

1. Cut a body and a head from brown paper, then cut four legs, an ear and a tail. Glue the pieces onto the big piece of paper.

2. Cut a pink shape for inside the ear and glue it on. Glue on a collar and eyes. Then, draw a nose and dots on the face.

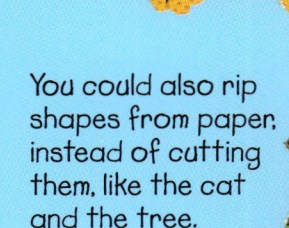

You could also rip shapes from paper, instead of cutting them, like the cat and the tree.

The grass in this collage was ripped from a page in a magazine.

Decorated pot

Spotted pot

1. Wash a terracotta flower pot thoroughly with water, to remove any soil. Then, leave the pot to dry out completely overnight.

Paint inside the top, too.

2. Paint the outside of the pot with white acrylic paint. Leave the paint to dry, then paint some light purple circles on the pot.

Make the circles different sizes.

3. Paint darker purple and yellow circles in the spaces. Then, paint more circles on top and leave the paint to dry.

Before you give the pot to your mum, put a pretty plant in it.

Press on leaf stickers from the middle of this book, around the flowers.

The spots on the pot above were fingerpainted.

Flowery pot

1. Wash a flower pot, let it dry, then paint it pale pink. Cut some circles and petal shapes from different colours of thin paper.

Use a glue stick.

2. Glue some of the petals onto the pot to make a flower. Then, glue a circle in the middle of the flower and add another flower.

The glue is clear when it dries.

3. Paint a thick layer of PVA glue all over the outside of the pot, including the flowers. Leave the glue to dry.

You could decorate a base, too.

Field of flowers painting

Use white or pale paper.

The paint needs to be runny.

1. Using a red wax crayon, draw some flowers near the bottom of a piece of paper. Draw some smaller ones further up the paper.

2. Add more flowers, using pink and yellow crayons. Then, pour some green paint onto an old plate and mix in some water.

3. Brush green paint over the flowers, to make grass. Then, paint the sky with blue paint. Paint stalks when the green paint is dry.

On Mother's Day, you could give your painting to your mum in a frame (see pages 30-31).

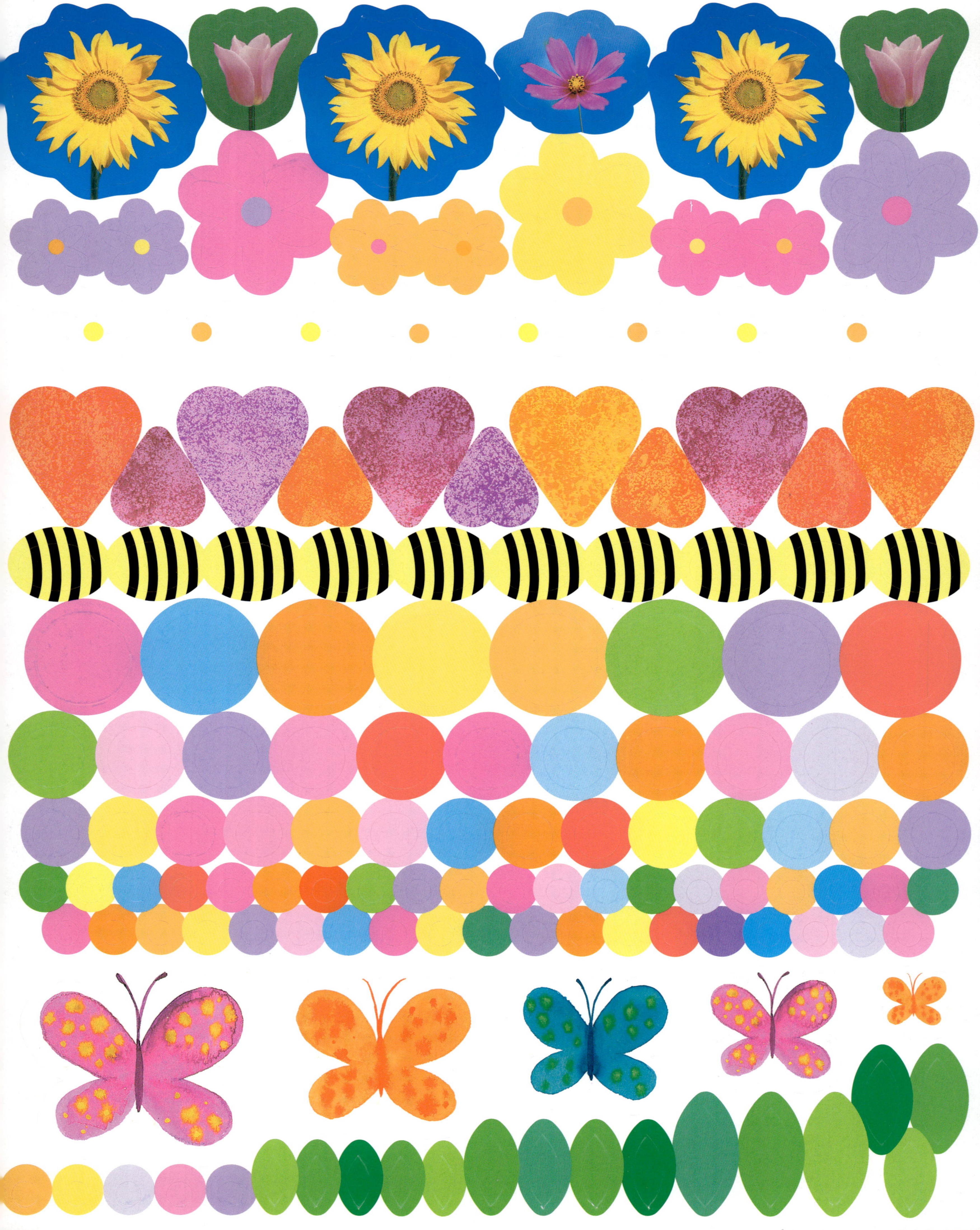

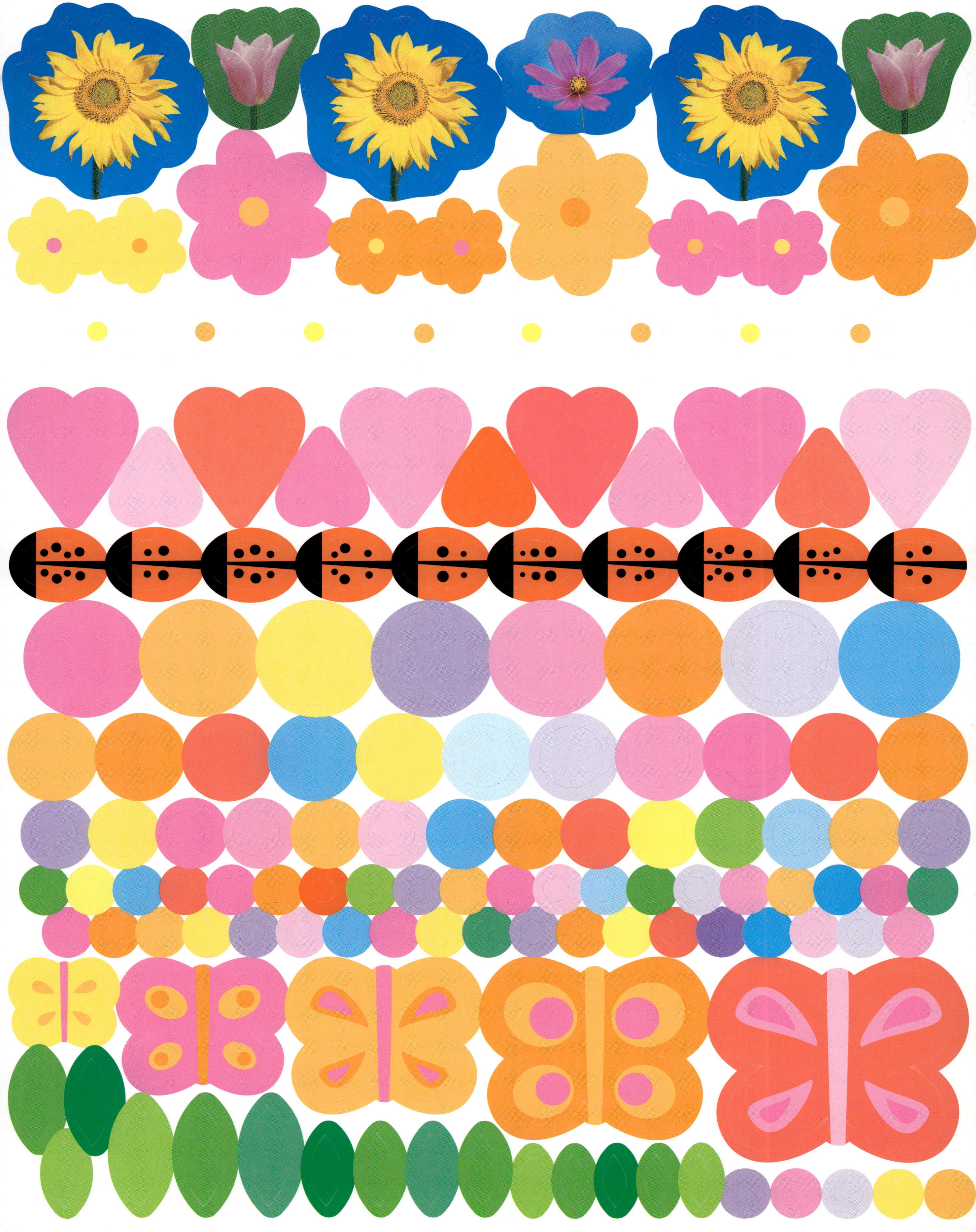

Printed wrapping paper

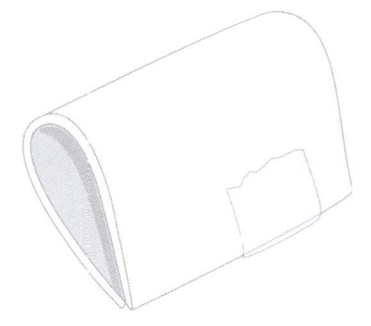

1. Cut a square of thick cardboard. Bend it around into a petal shape, then tape its edges together near the top.

2. Pour some paint onto an old plate and spread it out a little. Then, dip the bottom of the cardboard into the paint.

3. To print a flower, press the cardboard onto some paper, then lift it up. Print more petals. Then, print lots more flowers.

Dip the cardboard into the paint each time you print.

If you want to print a stalk, dip the edge of a piece of cardboard into some paint.

4. When the paint is dry, pour some yellow paint onto the plate. Fingerpaint middles for the flowers and let the paint dry.

Print the flowers on bright paper.

Flower chocolates

To make 12 flowers, you will need:

75g (3oz) white chocolate drops
3 tablespoons golden syrup
75g (3oz) plain chocolate drops

❁ These chocolates need to be stored in an airtight container in a fridge and eaten within a week.

These chocolates are shown bigger than real size.

1. Pour about 3cm (1in) of water into a pan. Heat the pan until the water bubbles, then remove the pan from the heat.

2. Put the white chocolate drops into a heatproof bowl. Then, wearing oven gloves, carefully put the bowl into the pan.

Use a wooden spoon.

3. Stir the chocolate until it has melted. Wearing oven gloves, lift the bowl out of the pan and leave it to cool for two minutes.

4. Stir in 1½ tablespoons of golden syrup until the mixture forms a thick paste which doesn't stick to the sides of the bowl.

5. Wrap the chocolate paste in plastic foodwrap. Then, melt the plain chocolate and stir in the rest of the golden syrup.

6. Wrap the plain chocolate paste in plastic foodwrap. Chill both pieces of chocolate paste in a fridge for about an hour.

7. Take both pieces of chocolate paste out of the fridge. Leave them for about 10 minutes, to soften a little.

8. Cut the plain chocolate into seven pieces. Then, wrap one piece in plastic foodwrap again and put it on one side.

9. Make the other six pieces into balls, then squash them a little. Smooth the edges of the shapes with your fingers.

10. Cut the white chocolate paste into seven pieces and make six smoothed balls, as before. Then, unwrap the plain chocolate paste.

Cool the paste in the fridge if it gets too soft.

11. To add flowers, roll small balls and strips of paste, for petals. Press a ball onto the middle of each one, then add petals.

Flowery boxes

You can use any small box to make a perfect present for Mother's Day. It can be used as a jewellery box or filled with gifts.

Rub the shapes, to flatten them.

1. Cut lots of shapes from bright colours of paper. Then, brush them with PVA glue and press them all over a box.

2. Cut lots of pictures of different kinds of flowers from old magazines. Cut as close to the edges of the flowers as you can.

3. Brush some PVA glue onto the back of one of the paper flowers. Then, stick the flower onto the top of the box.

4. Gently rub the flower, to make it really flat. Then, glue another flower onto the box, a little way from the first one.

5. Glue on lots more flowers. Glue some of them so that they go over the edges of the box, then press them down.

The glue will be clear when it dries.

6. Brush a thick layer of PVA glue over the whole box, including the flowers. Then, leave the glue to dry completely.

This was a round cheese box. It was painted and the flowers were stuck on when the paint was dry.

You could decorate the lid of a plain gift box.

For a yummy gift, fill a decorated box with lots of chocolate truffles (see pages 10-11).

Cut-paper card

1. Cut a large rectangle from some thick white paper. Then, fold the rectangle in half, like this, to make a card.

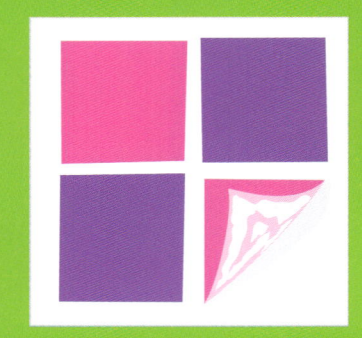

2. Cut four squares which are roughly the same size as each other from bright thick paper. Then, glue the squares onto the card.

3. Cut a pointed leaf shape from green paper, for one of the squares. Then, cut long thin stems and glue on all the pieces.

4. Draw a flower and cut it out. Then, cut out a middle, a stalk and a leaf. Glue the pieces onto one of the other squares.

5. From pink paper, cut out a strawberry shape. Then, cut out a stalk and small triangles. Glue them all onto the third square.

6. For the last square, cut a heart from bright paper. Then, cut another heart from some sponged paper and glue them on.

Sponged paper

The sponge makes a speckled pattern.

Pour some paint onto an old plate. Dip a sponge into the paint and dab it over a piece of paper, then leave the paint to dry.

Include pictures of things which your mum really likes.

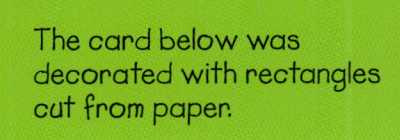

The card below was decorated with rectangles cut from paper.

Paper flowers

1. Draw around three round objects which are different sizes. Do each one on a different colour of thick paper.

2. Cut out the circles. Then, lay the middle-sized object in the middle of the biggest circle and draw around it.

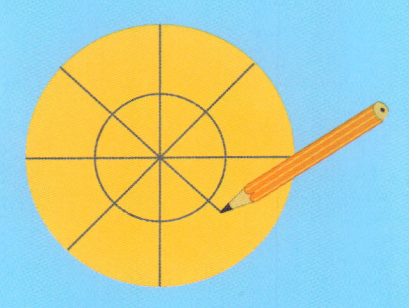

3. Draw a line across the big circle, then draw another line which crosses the first. Then, draw two more lines across them.

Decorate different jars with different paper shapes and stickers from the sticker pages.

4. Draw petals from the edge of the big circle to the edge of the middle circle, like this. Then, cut around the petals.

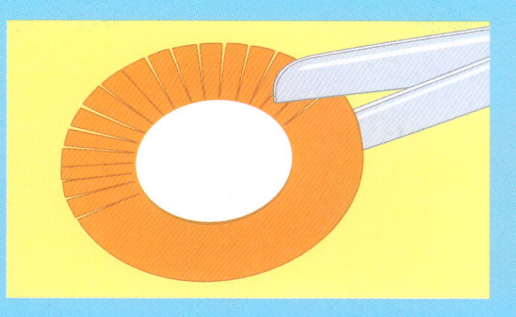

5. Glue the small circle onto the middle-sized one. Make lots of small cuts around the edge, as far as the small circle.

6. Glue the two smaller circles onto the big one. Add a stalk by taping one end of a drinking straw to the back of the flower.

A small jar will work best.

7. Press a piece of poster tack onto the other end of the straw and press it into the bottom of a clean glass jar.

This helps the stalk to stand up.

8. Scrunch up pieces of tissue paper and push them into the jar, around the stalk. Cut two paper leaves and glue them on.

Tiny decorated cakes

To make about 24 cakes, you will need:

1 medium egg
50g (2oz) self-raising flour
40g (1½oz) soft margarine
40g (1½oz) caster sugar
small paper cases
a baking tray

For the icing:
50g (2oz) icing sugar
about 1 tablespoon of warm water
pink food colouring
white writing icing, for decorating

Heat your oven to 180°C, 350°F, gas mark 4, before you start.

❁ These cakes need to be stored in an airtight container and eaten within four days.

Some of these cakes have two different layers of icing on them.

If you'd like to make white icing, don't add any food colouring.

Add a little more food colouring to make brighter pink icing.

Use a wooden spoon.

1. Break the egg into a mug. Then, sift the flour into a large bowl and add the egg, margarine and caster sugar.

2. Stir everything together well, until the mixture is smooth and creamy. Then, put 24 paper cases on the baking tray.

3. Using a teaspoon, spoon the cake mixture into the paper cases until each case is just under half full, like this.

The cakes will turn golden brown.

4. Bake the cakes for about 12 minutes, then carefully take them out of the oven. Lift them onto a wire rack and leave them to cool.

5. For the icing, sift the icing sugar into a bowl. Add the water and mix it in with a metal spoon until the icing is smooth.

6. To make the icing pink, add two drops of food colouring to the bowl. Then, mix it in well with a metal spoon.

7. Using a teaspoon, put a little icing onto the top of each cake. Then, spread out the icing with the back of the spoon.

You could decorate cakes with sweets or write letters on them, to spell out your mum's name.

8. Leave the icing for a little while to set. Then, draw decorations on the cakes, using the white writing icing.

Make the card from paper which matches some of the painted stripes.

Painted stripes card

1. Using orange paint, paint a thick line down a piece of white paper. Add two thinner lines, one on each side of the thick line.

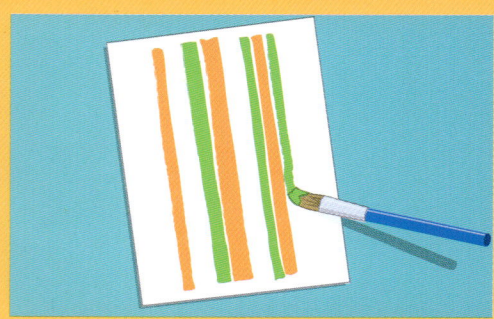

2. Paint a thick green line near the thick orange line, leaving a little gap. Add two thinner lines near one of the other orange lines.

3. Paint blue, pink and yellow lines in the spaces, so that you fill the paper, like this. Then, leave the paint to dry.

You can make the stripes go down or across the card.

There are lots of ideas for gift tags, including a striped one, on page 32.

4. Using a black felt-tip pen, draw dots on some of the stripes. Then, draw wiggly lines on some of the other stripes.

5. Paint pink blobs onto one of the orange stripes. Then, when the paint is dry, use a gold pen to add more spots, dots and lines.

6. Fold a piece of thick paper to make a card. Cut around the striped painting so that it fits on the card, then glue it on.

Shiny picture frame

1. Cut a large piece of kitchen foil. Using a glue stick, spread glue all over the non-shiny side, then fold the foil in half.

2. Rub the foil so that the two layers stick together and the surface is smooth. Then, put the folded foil onto an old magazine.

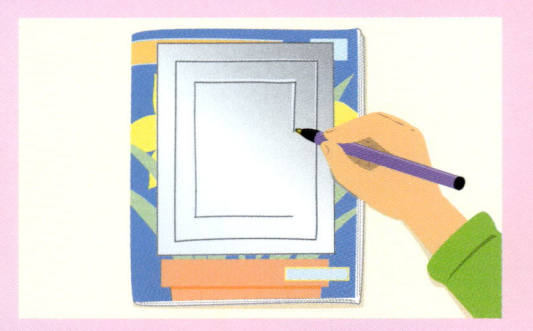

3. Pressing hard with a ballpoint pen, draw a rectangle on the foil, then draw a smaller rectangle inside it, like this.

4. Draw lots of flowers between the lines. Then, cut around the rectangles with scissors, a little way from the outside line.

5. Push a ballpoint pen through the foil, to make a hole for your scissors. Then, cut all the way around the inside line, to make a frame.

Don't worry if the edges aren't straight.

6. Lay the foil frame onto some thin cardboard and draw a bigger rectangle around it, like this. Then, cut out the shape.

7. Lay the foil frame onto the cardboard again and draw around the hole. Push a pen through the shape you've drawn.

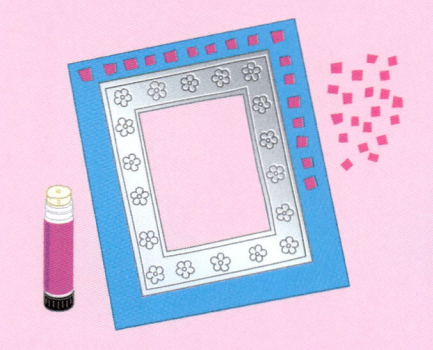

8. Cut out the shape, then glue the foil frame onto the cardboard one. Cut out lots of paper squares and glue them onto the frame.

9. Lay the frame on a picture, then turn them both over and tape the picture in place. Tape a loop of string at the top.

30

You could draw flowers and leaves on foil and cut them out separately.

Make a picture of yourself from paper (see pages 12-13) to go in the frame.

You could just put a photo of you in the frame, of course!

31

Gift tag ideas

You can use some of the techniques in this book to make gift tags. Here are some ideas you could try:

To make this tag, cut a striped painting (see pages 28-29) into strips and glue them onto a card.

You could print a flower and glue it onto a gift tag (see page 17).

To make a tag like this, cut out a flower (see pages 22-23) and glue it onto a small folded card.

To make a pretty gift tag, glue a painted butterfly (see pages 2-3) onto a yellow card.

You could glue a foil heart (see pages 30-31) onto squares of different-coloured paper, like this.

Find out how to make wrapping paper on page 17.

Series editor: Fiona Watt • Art director: Mary Cartwright • Photographic manipulation: John Russell
Images of flowers on the sticker pages and on pages 20-21 © Digital Vision.
This edition first published in 2008 by Usborne Publishing Ltd., Usborne House, 83-85 Saffron Hill, London, England. www.usborne.com Copyright © 2004, 2008 Usborne Publishing Ltd. The name Usborne and the devices ⚜ ⚜ are Trade Marks of Usborne Publishing Ltd. All rights reserved. No part of this publication may be reproduced, stored in a retrieval system, or transmitted in any form or by any means, electronic, mechanical, photocopying, recording or otherwise without the prior permission of the publisher. Printed in Malaysia.